YOU'LL SMILE AGAIN

FINDING LIGHT IN THE MIDST OF GRIEF

PAULINE MBURU, R.N.

GREAT
BOOKS

First edition

ISBN 978-0-578-97734-8

Typeset & Formatted by Roy Kamau - GREAT Books

"In the book "You Will Smile Again", the author Pauline N. Mburu, provides a comprehensive and detailed account of grief, sighting her own turbulent torrent of pain, grief, unforgiveness and fear. The book is so captivating and real, that when reading, one empathizes with the pain. Pain so vivid, you can almost touch and feel it. It is very therapeutic and a must read for parents like me who lost children under very similar circumstances, as it provides the means to deal with the loss. She explains the do's and don'ts when dealing with a grieving parent and appeals to the grieving to be kind to themselves and more importantly accept help or offer appropriate help as may be necessary."
Jane N. Clayton, M.Ed.

"A soul stirring journey of grief to acceptance, reminding every sojourner not to consider their own merit or worth, rather the grace poured forth by the Creator who enables us to smile once more despite the challenges death presents to us. A wonderful story of courage and hope."
Irene Chege, BSN/RN

"A must-read and a must-have-on-hand book. This book is encouraging to accept life and death and how to treat yourself during the grieving process. It's a reassuring book to help those that are grieving and to those that are in the grieving process. Beautifully written."
Pamela Lechuga, RN

"This book is very compelling and dynamic. The approach to its message is compassionate, warm and heartfelt. It gives one the courage and strength to accept and endure the losses of your loved ones."
Tanya Cheevers, M.D.
State of NC-DHHS-DSOHF

In Loving Memory

Wanjiru and Nduta, my darling daughters, without you, my entire world was rearranged.

The special memories of you will always bring the imagination of what you could have become. You both meant so much to us as a family and invariably you will. The fact that you both never stayed left us with a void, but you're forever tucked in our hearts forever until we meet again.

With some of the portions from this book, I would kindly like to build a bench with my daughters' names inscribed on it at the Mater Hospital in their memory. That is the place they were born and died. A request for permission has been sent to the hospital administration, whom I thank in advance.

Contents

Acknowledgement

To my parents, Mrs. Jane Nduta & Mr. Francis Mburu, thank you for the gift of life. I could not have had better parents than you. Your guidance and support throughout my life cannot be repaid.

To my siblings Joseph, Salome, Teresia, Sarah, Mary, Peter, George, John, and Simon. If I had an opportunity to pick my sisters and brothers, I would pick all nine of you. You all sure do add flavor to my life.

To my friends and family at large. I am forever grateful and thankful that our paths crossed. Your presence and support were a rainbow during my walk through the valley of the shadow of darkness.

To Janet Njanja and Sally Lubker, you came into my life and wonderfully became my daughters. I love you both unconditionally.

Dedication

I dedicate this book to my one and only surviving child, Nganga Kuria. When I look at you son, I am reminded of the goodness of life. You have done well in representing all the children that I was meant to have. I love you more than my words can express.

To the father of my children, Major Kuria Nganga, our son told me that he will always appreciate me for the person I chose to be his father. I echo the same feeling and I am thankful I had you in my life during those two calamities. I thank you!

Introduction

No valley is as vast as grief and no journey is as personal and life-changing as the death of a loved one, more so a child. All losses are unique in their own way, and we all share the loss of a truly special person(s). I happen to be in a different place than most. I lost my two daughters back-to-back. It was devastating and I thought I would never be able to go on with life again, but I did. Yes, I found my smile again.

In this book, I narrate my catastrophic experience related to the birth and death of my two daughters. My personal experience through the process of grieving with the hope that it will comfort you to know that you are not alone. Within this book, there is hope for a better tomorrow, because love makes the unbearable bearable.

I also offer what I learned during my grieving as it pertains to supporting someone in grief, the do's, and don'ts. There is no right or wrong way to grief, but there are appropriate ways to support a grieving person. This is based on my own experience as a bereaved parent and my experience as a registered nurse.

Grief is harder than our culture thinks and takes longer than the culture permits. It is less predictable and you have to go through it and learn to live with it as time goes by. Everyone's grieving path is different as such you will find what works for you through trial and error. Take it slowly and accept there will be some blind corners here and there.

To maintain the bond with your loved one is normal and how you conceptualize it depends on your own views on death and the afterlife. But no matter how you think about it, your loved one will always be in your memory. The goal isn't to break the bond with your loved one, but to live each day carrying that bond not as a burden, but as a gift with the hope of building a better tomorrow.

1

First Of Ten

I was born and raised in Naivasha, Nakuru County, Kenya. Like most African families that believed in large families, ours was not exceptional. I am the firstborn of ten children born of the same mother and father: five girls and five boys with one set of twins. Most commodities are shared in large families, and children learn to share whatever is available, which I consider a positive survival trait. My siblings and I learned this trait perfectly. We shared our homemade toys, and no one ate before confirming that each person had a portion.

The title of being the firstborn comes with responsibilities in Africa. In the absence of the parents, the firstborn takes over the parenting duties. Personal hygiene, cooking, and cleaning after all my nine siblings while my mother went farming or to the market was quite a task for me at times. I always told my mother how tiring it was to cater to several children.

My mother would say, *"it is only hard work when they are young kids."* She would add that having many children was a blessing and a delight once they are all grown. She would also say, *"who knows one of you might become a doctor, a teacher, a nurse, an engineer, a driver, a nun, or a farmer."* And that if any of us became a thug, *"there still would be someone to carry on the family name".*

My siblings are all adults now and in various professions, and thank goodness none of them became a *"thug."* We continue to share and cost-share the ups and downs of life, the same way we shared commodities when we were children. We participate in caring for our aging parents, whom we adore. We sure cherish each other more now that we are older. Really, I would not trade any one of my sisters or brothers for anything.

As a teenager, my wishful desire was to have two boys and two girls of my own when I grew up. The desire to have four children never came to fruition, for the cruel arm of death took my two girls and left me with my one and only son, of whom I am well pleased. I was very heartbroken with the loss of my two babies; hence I gave up on getting a fourth child due to fear of another loss.

2

As White As Snow

Growing up in Kenya where snow was only heard of, I was always puzzled when I would hear someone quote, "*as white as snow.*" My imagination of the snow being the whitest substance on the earth used to leave me in a wonderland. Upon my arrival in America in November 1998, I could not wait to see and experience the snow.

My new residence in my new country was in New York State, where they said that snow never failed to show up. December could not arrive soon enough for me to see the whitest substance from the sky. My imagination was going to come alive with the snow.

The weather forecast broadcasted the arrival of snow and I waited like a child on Christmas eve waiting to open their new toy. I peeked outside on and off throughout the day. As I was staring blankly out of the window, snowflakes started to trickle down from the sky in slow motion with a pearly white that I had never seen before. The snowflakes appeared pure and without a blemish. It was such a magnificent sight. However, upon hitting the ground, they instantly disappeared in front of my very eyes.

Suddenly, my mind was preoccupied with the thoughts of how my two beautiful babies landed in this world, at first innocent, and without a blemish but then they vanished, leaving us in shock, anguish, sadness, hopelessness, and helplessness. As I watched the snowflakes disappear and never to be seen again, I had a flashback of the birth and death of my two lovely babies. I no longer could enjoy the dancing snowflakes covering the trees. I quickly ran to my room and cried myself to sleep.

3

Nameless Birth

Mourning the death of a loved one is a process all of us go through at one time or another because death is inevitable. I wrote this book in memory of my two lovely daughters because my relationship with my girls did not end with their death. They remain tucked in my heart forever because when someone we love dies, we never get over it. We just slowly learn to go on without them but we always keep them tucked in our hearts.

My girls died nameless because the unforeseen tragedy extremely crushed their father and I, and naming them was the last thing in our minds. I here and now give my daughters their names according to the Kikuyu cultural child naming tradition. My first daughter is Wanjiru, named after my late mother-in-law and my second daughter is Nduta, named after my mother. I hope to utilize some of the profit from this book to build a bench at Mater Hospital with my daughters' names inscribed on it in their memory.

I wrote this book for you, the bereaved. Feeling gratitude for the gift of life might feel impossible during mourning. Kindly, I want you to know that you are not alone, for others have been where you are and have eventually been able to embrace life again. I am one of them. You and I are members of the same club. The club of those whose children and loved ones have gone before.

Secondly, I wrote this book for friends and family, for they play an exceptional role during bereavement by their presence and their support. The grieving family might not remember to thank you due to being emotionally unstable related to their loss. Kindly note they sincerely appreciate you more than words can express.

Thirdly, with this book, I would like to remind the medical professionals that they took an oath to save lives. Hence the need for compassion, a feeling of mercy, and a desire to help the suffering person. Empathy should be your internal badge, as in your heart and mind. Always put yourself in the victim's shoes and weigh how it would feel were you the victim. As a nurse and a victim, I have worn both shoes.

Finally, I encourage the leadership in health departments worldwide to do better. The hospital board and administrators have a noble job that requires going beyond the call of duty because the policies they put in place affect people directly and forever. Please aspire to see the bigger picture by thinking outside the box. Always put yourself in the patient's situation. I know you can do better.

4

Two Cruises

In October 2004, I was on a cruise from Orlando, Florida, to Bahamas Island. It was a lady's trip. Cruising has the pleasure of taking someone from a sheltered place to wider waters. It seems an ideal way for a break from work and the everyday routine. I consider it an ideal vacation where everything is within reach laterally. It is like a city in motion.

I was standing at the balcony of the Carnival ship cruising on the Atlantic Ocean. I was gazing at the ocean. The thought of leaving the water behind and never interacting with that same water again captured my mind. I got preoccupied with how my lovely daughters passed this world like water, never to be seen again. I felt unfortunate and guilty. Guilty of having not done anything to get known of what happened to my girls. The guilt of not letting the world know that there once were two lovely souls in this world who landed and departed soon after arrival.

Tears flooded my eyes. I wanted to walk to my cabin, but I was unable to. I felt weak. I sat down and supported my head with my hands, tears flowing down my chicks uninterrupted. It was then that I decided to write this book. However, my first few attempts were not successful because every time I sat to write, I was overwhelmed with sadness.

In February 2019, I was on another lady's trip, a seven days cruise to the Dominican Republic and Turks Island. While cruising on the Caribbean Sea, I was in one of the cafeterias sitting by the window eating my brunch. It was my time alone from the ladies. Looking through the window, I gazed at the water as it got propelled by the ship backward. I thought of how we cannot touch the same water twice because the passed flow will never pass again.

This made me feel sad and guilty of letting my daughters get forgotten like the passing waters. So, I decided to try again to write my book. I went to my cabin and brought some plain papers, a pencil and started the manuscript of this book. However, I ended up shelving it from being emotionally fatigued. Though I halted my writing, I promised myself that one day I would tell my story about how I battled my grief, and God will send my way the exact people who will need to hear this story for their own sake.

5

No Empathy

September remains the month that I would like to remove from the calendar if given the chance. My first daughter Wanjiru was born via cesarean section on September 4th, 1994, and died the same day. My second daughter Nduta was born via cesarean as well on September 11th, 1995, and died the same day. My birthday is September 13th, a birthday that I stopped celebrating after the death of my daughters. National daughters' day is celebrated in September. Needless to say, September became a trigger month for me related to my losses.

Thanks to social media, especially Facebook, which never fails to announce everyone's birthdays. This is usually followed by good wishes from friends and strangers alike worldwide. This is how I acknowledge my birthdays.

I attended my prenatal clinic religiously and with no issues during both pregnancies. The contractions began at term. It was time for baby Wanjiru to be born; hence my husband and I went to the hospital. I was admitted to the hospital, and my obstetrician was notified of my admission. I was in labor for a long time, waiting for my private obstetrician to arrive. I talked to the nurses and the intern doctor in the maternity ward. I was begging for surgery related to severe painful labor contractions with no advancement to delivery.

They explained that I had a personal private doctor and that with a private doctor, it was required of the individual doctor to authorize the hospital doctors to take over the patient. They explained that my doctor had told them that he was on his way. Hence, they had to wait for him per hospital policy. When it comes to maternity, personal or private doctors might not be a good option. I learned it through this dreadful experience.

The doctor finally arrived and found me in anguish with labor pains, and my baby was in distress. They performed an emergency cesarean section, but the umbilical cord was around the baby's neck, and the baby was gasping for air because the cord had been strangling her. Unfortunately, resuscitation was unsuccessful. I was in shock and slow to process that my baby had died. In fact, I kept pressing the call bell requesting the nurses to bring the baby to my room for breastfeeding. Unfortunately for me, they did not know how to tell me that my baby was gone. My husband had to bear the news to me after much frustration with the nurses who avoided my questions. Suddenly, I felt hollow and empty in that hospital room. The noise of the doctors passing by the hallway along with the heart monitors faded as I wished and hoped that I would awake from this nightmare with my baby in my arms.

When I was in nursing school, they taught us in Ethics class and Mental Health class about empathy and how to deliver bad news to a patient. They never taught us how to receive bad news ourselves in a situation where the deceased was our loved one. They did not teach us the intensity of such news. They never prepared us for the complete dissociation that a family member might experience but again they could never teach us that. No one can ever teach or describe the pain and disbelief of the loss of a loved one unless they experience it themselves. I know it now.

The day a nurse wheeled me to view the body of my baby, she was lying on a table naked, with no mark or any blemish on her beautiful body. She was intact but lifeless. Her lips, hands, and feet had turned to dark bluish discoloration. I was sitting in a wheelchair staring at her lifeless body sobbing uncontrollably when I suddenly lost consciousness. Upon regaining consciousness, I was in my hospital bed with blood linkage to the abdominal dressing from the cesarean section site. They had to reinforce the abdominal binder dressing.

At the time I lost my baby, my thought processing was surreal. The nurse should have taken the initiative to offer me the option of going with a family member or a friend to accompany me to view my child's body. Instead, she walked into my room with a wheelchair and said, *"I am here to take you to go see your baby."* I am not sure if she had a hard time using the words (the body of your baby). I think calling it what it was would probably have given me a reality check. I was in shock and not in a position to make decisions such as requesting a family member to come with me.

6

Unanswered Questions

A wife who loses a husband is called a widow.
A husband who loses a wife is called a widower.
A child who loses his parents is called an orphan.
There is no word for a parent who loses a child.
That's how awful the loss is.
– Jay Neugeboren—An Orphan's Tale, 1976.

The death of a child is the worst trauma a parent can endure because, in the birth order of nature, we expect our children to bury us and not vice versa. It is unnatural for a child to die before the parent. No word describes us. You and I are members of the same club: the nameless club. Parents whose children have predeceased them. A rare and very unfortunate club. Hence the need for us to join a grief support group where we offer emotional support to each other.

The level of pain that accompanies losing a child cannot be measured with a word or name, and losing a child is unfathomable. As a Christian, I struggled even to find Bible verses that apply explicitly to a parent losing a child. Which left me with a lot of unanswered questions like, Why me? Why my child? But again, if not me, why the other person? This is an experience that you would not wish on your worst enemy.

There was a desire to hang onto my babies, and the affirmation of their existence drove me into talking about them most of the time during the first few months of both incidents. It was the only thing that preoccupied and dominated my mind. There is no right or wrong way to grief. The truth is that the loss of a child is an ultimate human tragedy. No other loss comes close to exacting the huge emotional anguish that a child's loss elicits, and mourning never completely really ends. As such, there is a need to really show compassion, understanding, kindness, and patience to self.

I am incredibly sorry for your heartache, my fellow bereaved. I am sending you my love and comfort, and solace through this book. I have a lot of hope and reassurance that you will smile again after grief has taken its course. May you find comfort in the memories you shared with your loved one. There is always sunlight after darkness.

7

The First Nightmare

As I write this chapter, my eyes are blurry, and my throat chokes. I am reliving the moment that I was in that room with the baby Wanjiru's body. I was sitting in a wheelchair looking at my baby's body, questioning how God could allow a whole perfect baby to grow for nine months in my womb and only for her to die through strangulation from the umbilical cord moments after birth. Like what was the reason or rationale for it?

I wondered what I had done to deserve the painful loss. I prayed and begged God to revive my child to life. I begged God to resurrect my child back to life as he had done many years ago per biblical documentation. I was very desperate, and when no miracle occurred, my faith and belief in God were destabilized. I wrestled with questions related to God's existence.

Through my own experience, I learned anger is a natural part of grief and can be expressed in many ways, not necessarily by rage. Someone can be frozen by anger or sit still without speaking and maybe engulfed in anger. This happened to me when my personal obstetrician came to see me post-surgery, the day after baby Wanjiru's death. At that moment, I was lying in bed staring at the doctor in anger. I did not respond to him when he spoke to me. I thought of how I would have thrown that body to him and told him to take it as a trophy.

I finally left the hospital without a baby and with a cesarean section wound and very full uncomfortable breasts. As we departed the hospital, our son pointed at the hospital building and said, *"baby, baby."* He knew we were expecting a baby. I had told him that I would return home with a baby and that he was going to be a big brother. Our poor three-year-old son was trying to console me by holding my tummy and crying with me during the ride home. I am sure he was baffled and worried about why his mom was crying. I was very heartbroken and sad that I could not compose myself to explain why I did not have the baby. If anything, my son was too young to comprehend death. I wept my whole ride home.

Mentally, it was tough for me to get past that image of my dead baby. It was a vivid recollection; it was like a nonstop frozen frame of a movie in my mind. I used to have nightmares that did not scare me. Instead, I embraced my child in my dreams, holding her closer and caring for her, only to awaken up to nothingness and cry myself to sleep.

I felt trapped in a corner emotionally, feeling like there was nowhere to run. Life seemed too challenging to face. I just wanted to slam on the brakes and shut down completely, hoping the pain and anguish would just go away. I wished I could erase my child's entire episode of birth and death out of my mind but obviously, I couldn't. The intense desire to turn the clock back was overwhelming.

The struggle with expressing breast milk and pouring it out due to breast discomfort was a constant reminder of what had happened. I was feeling a big urge to fill the void of the loss. I thought it would help me move forward past the grief sooner and forget what I had gone through. So, I went ahead and became pregnant again to replace what had been robbed of me.

8

The Second Nightmare

The failure of my personal doctor to arrive on time and his failure to instruct the hospital doctor/s to take over his patient resulted in baby Wanjiru's death. I do not recall what his explanation was concerning his lateness. It did not matter anyway; a precious life had been lost related to his negligence.

I was in despair and I wanted justice. I needed to involve a lawyer, which was financially and mentally tasking and another stressor on my fragile state, considering I was pregnant. I decided to hold on from suing until after the new baby was born. My pregnancy was progressing despite the on and off emotional roller coasters related to grief.

I had to have an elective cesarean section surgery related to the history of the previous cesarean sections and to avoid any complications related to any delays considering the previous situation. I went back to the same hospital; I had delivered my firstborn child in the same hospital with no issues at all.

This was my 3rd cesarean section delivery, and the hospital was very aware of what had happened previously with baby

Wanjiru. They were all set to ensure that all would go well with this delivery. They had a private suit for me. All the medical professionals needed for this delivery were present which I sincerely appreciated.

My pregnancy was full-term, and baby Nduta was due for delivery. It was on September 11th, 1995, and the elective cesarean section was done. Surgery was timely and successful, but the baby's heart did not have one valve; hence, blood circulation could not circulate appropriately. An artificial valve needed to be placed in my newborn heart urgently. It was an emergency.

None of the hospitals in Kenya had performed heart surgery to a newborn. The only option at the time was to take the baby to South Africa. Per medical status and common sense, the baby could not have made it to South Africa. And again, my baby died while medical professionals watched helplessly and hopelessly.

I was frustrated and emotionally destroyed this time, not with the doctors, not with the hospital but with God. I felt God had failed me. I recall like it was yesterday when I was in that room where they had baby Nduta's body on a table. She looked intact from the outside. All the fingers and toes were in place. I wondered why God could not have utilized the tissues or muscles from one of the toes or fingers to create the missing valve.

Once again, it was deja vu. It was so hard to take and hard to grieve when the loss happened back-to-back. I experienced grief overload. I was an emotional wreck, wondering why my babies and why God would let a whole pregnancy grow to full term only to have an innocent baby die soon after birth. I wrestled with God, questioned just about everything that I had no doubts about him previously, like faith and life after death.

I questioned God's existence. I lost interest in going to church for several years. There would be no watching my girls grow, no proms, no graduations, no milestones to celebrate with my daughters. My emotions were everywhere questioning my beliefs and this is totally normal so don't be hard on yourself. You are human and you feel and reason like one at least in this life.

My faith is central to who I am. At this point, I believe God has a reason related to his doings, and his ways are not our ways, but in my humanness, I questioned him. I do believe in God, however, I think it is important for people to be authentic and not disguise their anger related to their loss because our feelings need to be heard with empathy.

9

Disoriented Emotions

eath is like an uninvited house guest that forces itself in our homes and never leaves; instead, it causes misery to the bereaved family. The grief of losing a child can be a nightmare. Our mind has a natural way of preparing us for the death of our elderly as they age. But we never expect our kids to die before us. Instead, we internally invest in our kids. We have a road map for them and their lives, and their early death turns our world upside down. Bereaved parents feel the highest intensity of crippling grief regardless of the age of the child and our sense of loss, sorrow, and longing are universal.

Grief is all the love you want to give your departed loved one but you cannot. So that unspent love gathers up in your eyes and flows out in tears, the lump in your throat and in that hollow part you feel in your chest. Most parents have a natural assumption that their children will outlive them, so a child's death brings a feeling of an everlasting wound because of the irreplaceable bond. The unique connection between you and your child, regardless of the age, you are devastated with pain and grief. Grieving parents can be confused, angry, disorganized, bitter, depressed, fearful, and frightened. We don't choose the way to grieve. Grief is a process that has to be done and we don't grieve like others, we grieve like our own self. Grief is as individual as a fingerprint. The feelings of despair and helplessness may last for a long time. The danger of losing your sanity is real, for the world you knew is swept from under your feet, and your expression of grief may feel like insanity because you are emotionally destabilized.

This I learned is a normal response to a traumatic shock. Grief disrupts you causing disorientation and confusion. Grief takes away your emotional defense, throwing you into unfamiliar territory. Even the simple tasks that you have always done automatically become very unfamiliar. I remember getting in the shower and standing there trying to figure out what to do. It made the water feel like a ton of bricks as I stood there in forced tears and cries of agony. I felt almost paralyzed at times.

During grief, actions that may be unsettling to others are a natural reaction to your loss and are part of the healing process. Be compassionate with yourself and your pain, loving yourself because you are deeply wounded, and that takes your total concentration. Your entire body and mind are focused on helping you to survive the process of grief, which is a long-term journey with no destination. Have faith that you will survive, and once again, you will enjoy the beauty of being alive and regain your smile.

The confusion and forgetfulness can be worrisome and sometimes embarrassing. However, your memory and concentration will eventually return. Mindfulness exercises can be helpful to ease tension and stress in the body and mind. In this exercise, you focus on your breathing, air getting in through your nose, and air getting out of you through your mouth. When your minds wander with intrusive thoughts, you try to guide your focus back to inhaling and exhaling, chest rising and chest going down.

Crying is a way in which your eyes speak when your mouth can't explain how broken your heart is. A warm compress across my eyes did soothe my tired muscles around the eyes related to stress resulting from crying. Attending to your emotional needs in the way that is right for you can be difficult because people who have never lost a child might think you are supposed to get over it and go back to work normally without crying on and off.

They might even stop asking how you feel because they assume you are alright. To them, everything is supposed to be okay, for your loved one is gone, and you cannot change it. Give yourself permission to feel the trajectory of emotions that come and deal with it in a manner that feels okay for you. However, look for moments of joy each day no matter how small, it will gradually become a habit.

Grief is a private experience; each process has its own uniqueness related to the relationship and the bond with your loved one. When you lose a child, you lose the connecting link experienced from the moment of your first bonding, whether it was at conception, at birth, or afterward. The depth of our grief is the measure of the heights of our love for our departed loved ones. Hence, expect the waves of grief to crash on the beach of life. No matter what your circumstances may be, life goes on and there is light at the end of the grief tunnel. Be patient and kind to yourself and you too will smile again. Grief is a release, a discovery, and a healing process. It is by the brain following the heart that we are able to release, discover and heal. It is the heart that aches when a loved one dies. As such it is our emotions that are most drastically affected. Our hearts blaze the trail through the thicket of grief.

10

The Detachment

It never occurs to any mother or parent that their child is going to die until after it happens. Then the mother becomes preoccupied with the thoughts of the possibility that another child could die. You may develop a heightened awareness of loss and life's fragility, and this may make you fearful and anxious.

Our son was four years old at the time of the second death. I developed a fear of losing him too, and I wrestled with it most of the time. Much later, I realized that I unintentionally detached myself from our son which I later came to understand was a protective mechanism related to the fear of going through the same painful experience again. The discovery of how fragile life can be made me very fearful for my son. Obviously, I wanted him to have a good life with a healthy mother who was cheerful and pleasant as prior to the loss of his sisters. It was during the detachment that I relocated from Kenya to the US, then reunited with him later on.

Surviving children feel overwhelmed by their parent's grieving. They want to know their parents are stable and will be there for them. You will need to make a decision that your life is worth living despite sorrow and grief. No matter what the circumstances you may find yourself in, kindly consider the lives involved or affected by your decisions. Committing suicide to join your beloved one is not an option.

I used to feel very concerned and worried for any pregnant women I saw, for I knew what happened to me could befall them. I stopped attending baby showers because they used to reignite the memories of the deaths of my children. While everyone would be excited about the pregnancy at the baby shower, my mind would get preoccupied with concerns for the mother and the unborn baby.

We live in an unpredictable world. Where unexpected bad things happen to anyone related to laws of nature. Therefore, for anything that is beyond our control like death. We have no choices other than to accept the situation and be of benefit by reaching out to others. We learn through both good and bad experiences. It is my hope that my unfortunate experiences will bring you hope and help you to cope with your grief. The most powerful thing we can offer each other during mourning is companionship.

I experienced compound grief and survived the double loss of my babies. Hopefully, my story can be an encouragement to you or someone that you might gift them this book during their season in the valley of the shadow of darkness. There is light at the end of the grief tunnel and you will smile again. In case you might not hold any faith, we grieve because we love our children. Love is a constant thing in the grieving and healing process. Seek love for it helps to survive your loss and to cope with the pain. Take care of yourself, your feelings, and your body. Do everything in mindfulness to relax your body and mind and to help reduce stress.

11

Restoration

Upon relocating to North Carolina from New York in 2015, I met Janet at a church service, and later I met Sally at North Carolina state fairgrounds. These two young ladies became part of my life each in their own ways.

Interestingly they don't know each other. They not only looked up to me but also looked out for me. They'd call and text me out of blue, just to check on me or to ask my opinion. Our interactions are similar to that of a mother and daughter.

Sally gets into my personal affairs by asking very personal questions and voicing her opinions genuinely. She offers to take me shopping just so that I don't buy clothing that is not in fashion for particular occasions.

I have an online business, shoppokeasifa.com, and occasionally, I attend events and sell items in person. Without me asking for help, Janet volunteers at my selling events and takes charge just like a daughter would and she refuses payment for the labor and time spent.

These two young ladies will not watch me walk with a speckle on my face or with my hair out of place and I truly appreciate their kindness because it's the little things that matter most.

Janet and Sally, you have no idea how wonderful you both are to me. You became the daughters I was meant to have and you both have made my world a better place. May God guide you, keep you safe and give you everlasting peace, love, and joy.

12

The Fog of Guilt

Bereaved parents feel an overwhelming sense of remorse. If only, should have, would have, could have become unavoidable questions. "If only I used a different doctor ..." was one of mine when Wanjiru died. I experienced some feelings of guilt, thinking that the father of my children and I might have done something wrong and that the children were taken from us as a punishment.

I consulted with my mother, trying to find out if any traditional or cultural rituals that could have been done or not done that might be related to the loss. My mother reassured and comforted me. Her explanation that it was all in God's will, did not make any sense to me either. I said, *"Mother, my babies were innocent, and they died for no fault of their own."* Why them? Whose sins were they punished for? This was a question that used to go round and round in my thoughts.

My father reminded me of a verse in the Bible that says, *"As he passed by, he saw a man blind from birth. And his disciples asked him, 'Rabbi, who sinned, this man or his parents? He was born blind?' Jesus answered, 'It was not that this man sinned or his parents, but that in him the works of God might be displayed in him.'"* *John 9:1-14.* At this point, I could only hope that my babies did not die in vain.

I have since learned that the feeling of guilt does not mean you are responsible for your loved one's death. Instead, guilt and the pain that death brings are a fundamental part of the grieving process. It might take a while to get over these feelings, but with time they will ease. There is no context to place the death of a child, as it is most unexpected.

Most likely, you might feel angry. I was angry more so with the doctor for his absence and his late arrival. I was upset with the hospital for not performing the good Samaritan act. Questions spanned round in my head, repeatedly like a stuck record player. 'If only I could have used a different doctor etc.' I had many questions but no answers but regret and remorse.

The despair and helplessness behind my questions, the feelings of loss of control, self-blame with weird thoughts like; I could not have made a good mother to my girls, Which I related to a simple thought like my lack in not knowing how to braid hair. There is no timetable that tells someone's brain when to quit thinking of these unanswered questions. Those thoughts will stop when they no longer serve your grieving process. Meanwhile, someday, you the bereaved, will see with clarity, but during the first months of grief, things could be foggy.

Guilty or not, your errors can no longer be amended. Now is not the time for fruitless recrimination because whatever shame or guilt you feel serves no purpose. What you need most are gentle memories. You have to be willing to push forward with determination for a better tomorrow and dare to move forward faithfully. Rely on all the strength you have inside.

Stay in touch with those who touch your life with love. Let loose the sparkle and keep your spirits up by going with the transformation. Be available to help other grieving persons. This is deeply comforting and offering a smile is an act of kindness.

Life is made up of little things in which kindness and smiles are what preserve the heart. It is not uncommon for bereaved parents to suppress a smile by holding onto pain from the broken heart. As we begin to live again and move forward with our life. Most often people feel that in appearing happy, they are betraying their departed loved ones. So instead of denying our feelings, we should pay attention to our needs.

13

Forgiveness

I walked through the valley of the shadow of darkness and experienced the pain and anguish of grief. I had a lot of bitterness towards the doctor due to his lateness and failure to instruct the hospital accordingly. I was angry towards the hospital, for I believed they could have delivered the baby through good Samaritan Law (which offers legal protection to people who give reasonable assistance to those in peril). I was annoyed towards God. It was difficult reconciling with what had happened to my babies.

I grew up knowing that God could perform miracles, as exemplified by the many miracles documented in the Bible, especially raising people from the dead. I prayed and called upon Him to revive my children back to life. I was bitter towards God; I questioned God's existence, and for Him to let the worst thing happen and expect acceptance felt like a hideous thing to do during my initial period of grief. I could not maintain my faith in God for a couple of years after the second baby's death. You too may struggle to maintain your spiritual beliefs and practices.

Keeping faith can be difficult because the loss of your loved one aggravates you. I quit asking why when there were no answers. However, grief is like glitter whereby when a handful is thrown in the air when you try to clean it up, you will never get it all cleaned. Even long after the event, you will still find glitter tucked in the corners. Bitterness is part of grief but do not let it control you or your actions.

When I realized that I could not take God to court and hold Him accountable for the missing valve in baby Nduta's heart and her death, I forgave the doctor for his lateness. I forgave him to an extent that I would have difficulty identifying him in a lineup. I forgave the hospital for failure to act related to their policies. I hope they evaluated and adjusted their policies so that they can act accordingly should a situation like the one that happened to me occur to someone else, as relates to the absence of a patient's private doctor.

More importantly, I forgave so that I could regain freedom from negative thoughts, emotions, and stress-related symptoms. Forgiveness yields peace, reconciliation and generally promotes wellness by letting go of the resentment and the desire for revenge. We forgive to live without the bitterness or anger of the person that wronged us. The ultimate remedy for irritation is forgiveness, so find a place in your heart that can open to forgiveness, including self-forgiveness.

Forgive yourself for any unfinished business that you could or should have done before your demise. Be patient about unsolved concerns in your heart and allow yourself permission for not knowing how to maneuver the unknown, for with time you will find a sustainable way to move forward without noticing it. Be compassionate with yourself and your pain, loving yourself without self-blames. Forgiving yourself when you feel unreliable and unable to pay attention as you previously did.

Having spent part of my life either reliving the past unintentionally or trying to experience my future before it arrives, I realized that in between these two extremes is peace that can be sustained by forgiving others. Forgive others, not because they deserve it but because you deserve peace.

Forgiveness is letting go of the pain. It is also choosing to learn the lessons that have been produced from the incident. We accept what has happened because it will not change.

Forgiveness allows us to move forward. I know firsthand the comfort and strength that come from forgiveness. I obtained my life and my smile back. Nevertheless, forgiveness is the opposite of resentment and revenge. To forgive does not mean to overlook the need to right the wrong. Forgiveness and justice are both essential to healing.

14

Transformation

C alamities can happen to any of us in this life. What is most important is dealing with the process, coping with the changes, and getting through to the other side where the sun is still shining. I realized that time itself is part of the healing process. Grief is not something you get over in a week. You cannot go around it, you must go through it. Some people grieve quietly and some grieve loudly. Find the way that feels best in your heart. However, with time, transformation will occur whereby your current suffering will change to be less frequent, less intense, and shorter in duration. The excruciating pain changes over time to a dull ache with the recurring images decreasing with time. During your grief, you might have a hard time believing that you will build a life with new meaning, which you will as time goes by.

One thing I know for sure from my own experience is that grief keeps its own schedule. It will get easier and you will be able to remember the good times. But for now, it is understandable to think of your beloved more often than anything else. So, if you find yourself preoccupied with thoughts of your beloved, it is okay even though you know that your loved one is physically not there anymore. The death of our loved ones transforms us so profoundly that when we begin to emerge into the world. We do so in honor of their lives in the knowledge that grief is love. Take each minute as it comes.

I cried to God to revive my baby back to life even after one whole week of my child's death. I still imagined the hospital calling us with the news that our baby had risen to life despite the impossibility. Whatever feelings you may experience, anger, hostility, bitterness, etc. allow them to be felt because if you ignore them, they will show up in other ways, and they can be emotionally draining.

You might experience emotional numbness. Which people mistake for nothingness. Numbness is not the absence of feelings. It is the response to being overwhelmed by too many feelings which actually happens to some people during grief. It provides a protective defense. It is a temporary protection from emotional or physical pain. Be kind to yourself for kindness in thinking creates profoundness.

Honestly, only those that have lost a child or a loved one can understand. At least they can relate to your pain through their own experience. One might look normal, but from the inside, you know it is not you anymore. People besides you cannot see the terrible wounds inside because the trauma is invisible to others. This grief may create a disconnect between you and others, leading to a feeling of isolation causing more emotional pain.

I did not have the privilege of connecting with other bereaved mothers because I was never referred to any compassionate groups at that time, and I never knew of any grief support groups. I am not sure if they were such groups in my country Kenya at that time, but at least now they do have some.

I now reside in the USA, where group therapies are prevalent and encouraged. I joined a grief support group, and I have learned through personal experience that such groups are truly beneficial. They offer emotional support and acknowledgment to the bereaved. The bereaved get an outlet to vent their struggles and experiences to people that can relate with them. To hear stories that others have experienced is, in a way, reassuring. It reminds you that you are not alone in your loss. With current technology, someone can join grief support groups online worldwide. I encourage support groups.

15

The 5 Stages of Grief

Grief is an intense, overwhelming emotional sadness related to the loss of a loved one. Feeling numb and removed from daily life, unable to carry on with regular duties while saddled with their sense of loss is a natural reaction to loss. Grief is universal but has a personal experience to it. Individual experience of grief varies and is influenced by the nature of the loss.

Mourning is full of conflict and oscillation between resolution and regression. Coping with the loss of a loved one requires healing, and healing is a journey with no shortcuts through the stages of grief. Experts advise those grieving to realize they cannot control the process and prepare for varying grief stages. Looking back, I did experience the five stages of Grief per Elisabeth Kubler Ross Swiss, an American psychiatrist. These stages are Denial, Anger, Bargaining, Depression, and Acceptance.

It is important to know that they are not experienced linearly or in uniform. I had a trajectory of emotions that cycled over and over along with compound grief. It was an emotional rollercoaster with unpredictable highs, lows, and setbacks. Grief does not always unfold in an orderly or predictable manner. The stages of grieving are very organic, and they propel us in moving forward in relation to healing.

Living with grief can be lonely with or without a spouse. Even when you have other family members since each person has a unique relationship with the person that is lost. I had a feeling of emptiness and loneliness despite the presence of family and friends. Families that acknowledge the death of their loved ones and talk about it openly may be less negatively affected by the death. Understanding why they are suffering can help to talk and try to resolve issues that cause significant emotional pain, such as feeling guilt or self-blaming for a loved one's death.

This can create a healthy space for venting anger and resentment in a family. It can increase closeness and togetherness because you will get to understand what each family member feels related to the loss, and this will help in moving forward as a family. It is a matter of the heart and soul.

Mourning can last for weeks or months. Pain gets tempered as time passes and as the bereaved adapts to life without a loved one. There is a need for you to recognize the red flags and reach out to someone to talk about your concerns. As a nurse, I suggest that if you are uncertain about whether your grieving process is normal when you get depressed and don't want to get out of bed, consult a healthcare professional. It is not something to be ashamed of. Just like we seek medical attention when we contract an infection, likewise, we should do what needs to be done for emotional suffering.

This will help prevent you from getting into complicated grief, which is a heightened state of mourning that keeps someone from healing. Outside help from a mental health professional is beneficial to your recovery as you heal.

16

Words to Avoid

The truth is death destabilizes our mind and at times interferes with the thinking process, especially during the initial stages of grief when one is still in shock and denial. **The grieving person needs you and not the explanations of justifying death.** They are shocked and miss their loved ones, and feel the void in their life. As such, statements could be misinterpreted while you may say them with good intentions.

Here are some comments to avoid:

- **"It is well".** No, it is not well. The wearer of the shoe knows where it pinches. Life lost is not replaceable, and that hurts.

- **"Are you okay?"** Obviously, they have lost a loved one. Who could be okay after such a loss?

- **"Don't worry, he/she is with the Lord."** Telling them how much their death is better in Lord's sight is not helpful at all. Not all that share that belief.

- **"Look at what you should be thankful for."** Of course, they know they have things to be thankful for, but right now, that is not important at all. They could give it all out to get their loved ones back to life.

- **"He or she is in a better place."** Keep your beliefs to yourself unless asked. Some people do not believe in life after death or hell or heaven.

- **"We prayed for him to get well; however, the Lord has provided him with eternal healing."** This may sound twisted and confusing to someone whose pain of the loss is still fresh and overwhelming.

- **"She or he lived a long life, and most people die young."** Regardless of the deceased's age, death is a life lost and causes emotional agony to the bereaved.

- **"I understand how you feel."** Every death is felt differently by the grieving persons depending on their bond with the deceased. Please do not claim to understand how they feel.

17

Supporting a Grieving Person

T o comfort a grieving person. Never underestimate the comforting effect that comes with a hug, a kind word, or an ear to listen. If you have never lost a loved one, it will be difficult to understand what it is like to wade through the jungle of grief. You should imagine yourself in the shoes of your bereaved one because only by imagining that, can you begin to transform sympathy to empathy.

Empathy allows you to understand a fraction of the anguish and pain. Even though you will never fully comprehend what life is like without a loved one, you will empathize and show love to a grieving person without being judgmental.

My family and I sincerely appreciated every thoughtful action and kind word we received at the time. Truly some well-meaning people don't know what to say to a grieving person. They may feel pressure to say something that will fix the pain to the grieving person. Many people think their comfort wording related to death should make a grieving person shout for joy. Kindly note, you do not need to have answers or to give out-of-the-ordinary advice.

Now more than ever, the bereaved needs your support. Kindly note, there are no magic words that will make one feel better at that time. Nothing you say can take away the pain one experiences from losing the most precious person in their life. You can't justify death, but a hug shows you understand the pain.

The most comforting thing is to show your empathy that you are genuinely sorry for their loss. Here are a few tips that I learned in nursing school and from my own personal experience during my own loss.

The most important thing you can do for a grieving person is to be there. It is your support and caring presence that will help them to cope with the pain and gradually begin to heal.

Acknowledge the situation and express your concern. *"I am sorry to hear of your loss,"* or *"I am sorry to hear your so and so died."* It is okay to mention the deceased. It is reassuring to the bereaved that their loved one is not forgotten.

Ask how they feel. The emotions of grief can change rapidly, so do not assume you know how the bereaved person feels at any given time. One day the grieving person may want to cry on your shoulder. On another day, they may want to vent or sit in silence, or share memories. Simply being there and listening to them can be a huge source of comfort and healing.

Let the bereaved talk about how their loved one died. People who are grieving may need to tell the story repeatedly. Repeating the story is a way of processing and accepting and with each retelling, the pain lessens. By listening compassionately, you are helping them in healing.

Maintain support after the funeral. The majority leave the bereaved after the funeral, and this is a very lonely period when the void of the deceased is really felt by the grieving person. Call them often.

Offer practical assistance and help in practical ways. Everyday tasks are enormous for someone in grief. Offer to shop for groceries or run errands. Drop off ready-made food. Take care of the housework. Babysit their children or pick the children from school. Take their kids to the park or to an event to give the parents a break. No need to ask them what you can do to help. Just do it because they might not be in a position to figure out what needs to be done.

Encourage them to join a support group. Provide ongoing support over the long haul. Do not make assumptions based on outward appearances. The pain of bereavement never fully heals. Offer extra support on special occasions like death anniversaries when triggers mostly occur.

18

Guide To Surviving Grief

The reality of loss is that grief is both physically and emotionally exhausting. It is irrational and unpredictable. When someone we love leaves this life, it is important to remember the loss and pain are unexplainable, unimaginable, and almost unable to bear another day without them. The hardest part of healing after you have lost someone you love is to recover the "you" that went away with them. It feels like you may die of a broken heart when you lose a loved one.

Grief moves at a certain pace and what is lost cannot be restored, and you are in pain that cannot be made better. The reality of grief is far different from what others see from the outside. There is pain that you cannot be cheered out of and you do not need solutions. You need someone to hold your hands while you stand there in horror, staring at the hole that was left by the cruel death.

Some things cannot be fixed because when someone you love dies, everything in your world changes. What many do not understand is that we grieve all the things they missed and will miss. We grieve the life we lost and the future we expected to have together, and the list goes on.

Grief is to be witnessed and not to be fixed. People feel like they need to do or say something to fix your grieving situation. Nothing they can do or say will change the situation. Grief is not a fixable situation. It is a passage and you have to go through it. The best they can do is be present and offer a hug or a shoulder to cry on.

My fellow bereaved person, sleep or take naps as often as you can. Sob in the shower, take a mindful stroll looking at nature, release your pain without fear; Sing or listen to music; Cry or vent whenever you need to and eat a little something at least a couple of times a day. Meditate if you are a meditator or engage in relaxing activities.

I used to find myself talking about my babies to those that came to visit me sometimes repeatedly. Now, I know it was a way of venting and letting the pain out of my mind and heart. I sincerely appreciate those who sat and listened to me quietly.

Grief makes a person understand how fragile life is and it changes us. The pain sculpts us into someone who understands more deeply, hurts more often, appreciates more quickly, and cries more easily. Hopes more desperately and loves more openly.

The Serenity Prayer
"God, grant me the serenity to accept the things that I cannot change, courage to change the things that I can, and Wisdom to know the difference."

The serenity prayer is reported to have been written by theologian philosopher Reinhold Niebur for a Sunday service in

Heath, Mass, in 1937.

In other words, God gives us the grace to accept with serenity the things that we cannot change. Courage or the willpower to change the things that are changeable and the knowledge to distinguish one from the other, the changeable and not changeable situations. In a situation where you cannot change the outcome, then your only option is to accept it as is because it is out of your hands. Death is one of the unchangeable. Acceptance is the heart's best defense because you will find the serenity within to let go of the worst and find hope inside that continues throughout life. Acceptance is the only option in unchangeable situations.

Positive thinking is a habit and we can practice it until it becomes second nature to us. This will help you gain pleasure within your soul that no worry or hardship can take away. I learned that repeating a positive thought in one's mind can replace a negative thought. As such, I recite the serenity prayer as often as possible. Reciting this prayer has been invaluable in calming the storms related to the overwhelming grief and in helping me to refocus on matters related to life storms. The serenity prayer has carried me through daily living and continues to sustain me spiritually in various aspects of life.

You might think it could be depressing, but honestly, it is uplifting to hear people's stories of love and strength. People need a place where they can be open and honest about their grief without being judged. Hence, the reason for joining a grief support group is that you will be in the company of others who have been through the valley of the shadow of darkness like you. Hence, they are more likely to understand you from the depth of the emotions you are experiencing.

19

Triggers

A trigger is a reminder of past trauma. This reminder can cause a person to feel overwhelming sadness, anxiety, or panic. It may also cause someone to have flashbacks, which is a vivid, often negative memory. It can cause someone to relive a traumatic event. Progression of grief from the excruciating first days through the long-term healing where grief never really ends. We naturally adapt to living without our departed ones, but they remain tucked in our hearts forever.

With my broken heart, I learned to move forward, embrace life, and smile again. Grieving is not a journey, for there is no destination. The loss of a child is a loss of part of you because you and your child share a deep identity. Regardless of your child's age at death, you have lost a part of yourself that cannot be regenerated hence the grief of a child is timeless.

I am appreciative of the subconscious mind for its function of storing away the memory of the catastrophic loss of my daughters. Otherwise, life would be unbearable if thoughts of the life and death of my babies remained constant in my conscious mind. I do not think of my experience daily unless triggered by situations like September, which is the anniversary of both incidents.

"How are your kids?" *"How many children do you have?"* I struggle with the responses to such questions because my mind wonders by responding that I have one child, feels like I am not acknowledging my daughters, and obviously, I cannot respond that they are okay. Baby showers, too, reminded me of my own two cesarean sections and no baby to show. Most often, I send my gift instead of attending the baby shower events in person.

My father lost his brother, his best friend while conversing with him during the mourning. He told me that death wears more heavily on most people because as much as it is inevitable, the majority of people are mostly caught unawares by the death of their loved ones. He explained that we should try to live a life with an expectation of the arrival of death anytime, and by doing so, we would not be struck too heavily by the loss when it occurs.

20

Conclusion

The reality is that you will not get over the loss of your loved one, but you will learn to live with it. You will heal and you will rebuild yourself around the loss you have suffered. You will be whole again but you will never be the same. Grief should be allowed to take its own course, which differs from one person to the other. Grief is a natural process, and "recovery" cannot be rushed. Take as much time as you need.

It involves learning to cope and to build a life with new meaning. I am hopeful that you will find a way to deal with your grief so that you can return to living life. Meanwhile, take it one day at a time. The void left by your loved one will be your new reality, and you will need to find a way to live in a way that fulfills you.

My thoughts are with you. For most people, it will always hurt, but we need not let that consume us. At some point, you will need to let your love for your loved one outshine the loss of them. We have to keep moving forward in pursuit of life's challenges because by not moving forward; you risk slipping backward with grief complications. However, it is about an internal change that occurs gradually when grief has taken its cause.

Accepting the reality that your loved one is physically gone and recognizing the new reality of living without them is the permanent reality. We will never replace what has been lost but we can make new connections. By listening to our needs, we can evolve and invest in new relationships by reaching out to others and becoming involved in their lives. Your smile awaits.

One of the most remarkable skills in this life is to enjoy the good times even when life is not so great. We should live every day to the fullest in honor of our departed ones because they no longer have the option. However, we cannot do so until we have given grief its time. As such, be patient with yourself by taking one day at a time. May you find comfort in the memories you shared with your loved one.

Compassion & Support

Complicated grief can occur due to a lack of intentional support during grief, which is needed soon after the loss. In a time like this when people are losing several loved ones in short periods of time related to the Pandemic, people may experience compounded grief also known as cumulative grief. Which is a pile-on effect of grief or grief overload.

Losing several loved ones in a short period of time does not allow time to heal from one grief to the next. Hence, the grief keeps piling on top of each other and this causes a downward spiral and a bereaved person could hit the rock bottom.

It's difficult to heal or cope when you are trying to heal from multiple incidents. As such you should seek professional help; it is your first step in helping yourself towards healing.

The Tears Foundation is an international organization that brings hope and compassion to families across the **nation and globally.** This is a nonprofit organization that seeks to compassionately lift a financial burden from families who have lost a child. They provide funds to assist with burial or cremation services to families in need.

They also offer the parents comprehensive bereavement care in the form of support groups and peer companions. This foundation helps bereaved families honor the life of their children. You can reach this foundation via http://www.th etearsfoundation.org

The Tears foundation also offers free **emotional support groups** for families who have experienced the death of their children. You can reach them via emotionalsupport@ thetearsfoundation.org.

Grief Support Group and Grief Support Universal #GSU are online Facebook groups that provide platforms for bereaved persons to share freely.

About the Author

As a registered nurse and a mother, Pauline Mburu has touched many lives through her harrowing experience of losing two daughters. Her life's mission is to comfort and encourage many through what might be the most difficult time of their lives. Professionally, she has worked in various health care facilities both in Kenya and North America. She currently resides in the US impacting lives each day. Connect with her more at www.smileagainbook.com.

You can connect with me on:
- ◑ https://www.smileagainbook.com

9 780578 977348